THE HISTORY OF THE INCA EMPIRE

History of the World

Children's History Books

Speedy Publishing LLC

40 E. Main St. #1156

Newark, DE 19711

www.speedypublishing.com

Copyright 2017

The Inca had the largest empire in South America before the Europeans arrived. Who were they, and how did they rise so high? Let's find out!

VIEW OF THE LOST INCAN CITY OF MACHU PICCHU

A GREAT EMPIRE

At its most powerful point, the Inca Empire ruled most of the west of South America between what is now Ecuador and Chile. Millions of people lived in the empire, from the great capital city of Cuzco to little villages high in the mountains.

WHERE THE INCA CAME FROM

The Inca claimed that they came from an earlier civilization, the Tiwanaku, which had its territory around Lake Titicaca. Historians believe that they came more directly from the Wari Empire, and its regional center of Chokepukio, around 1000 CE.

SPECTACULAR VIEW OF THE UROS ISLAND AND
THE BOATS ON THE LAKE TITICACA, PERU

TIWANAKU RUINS

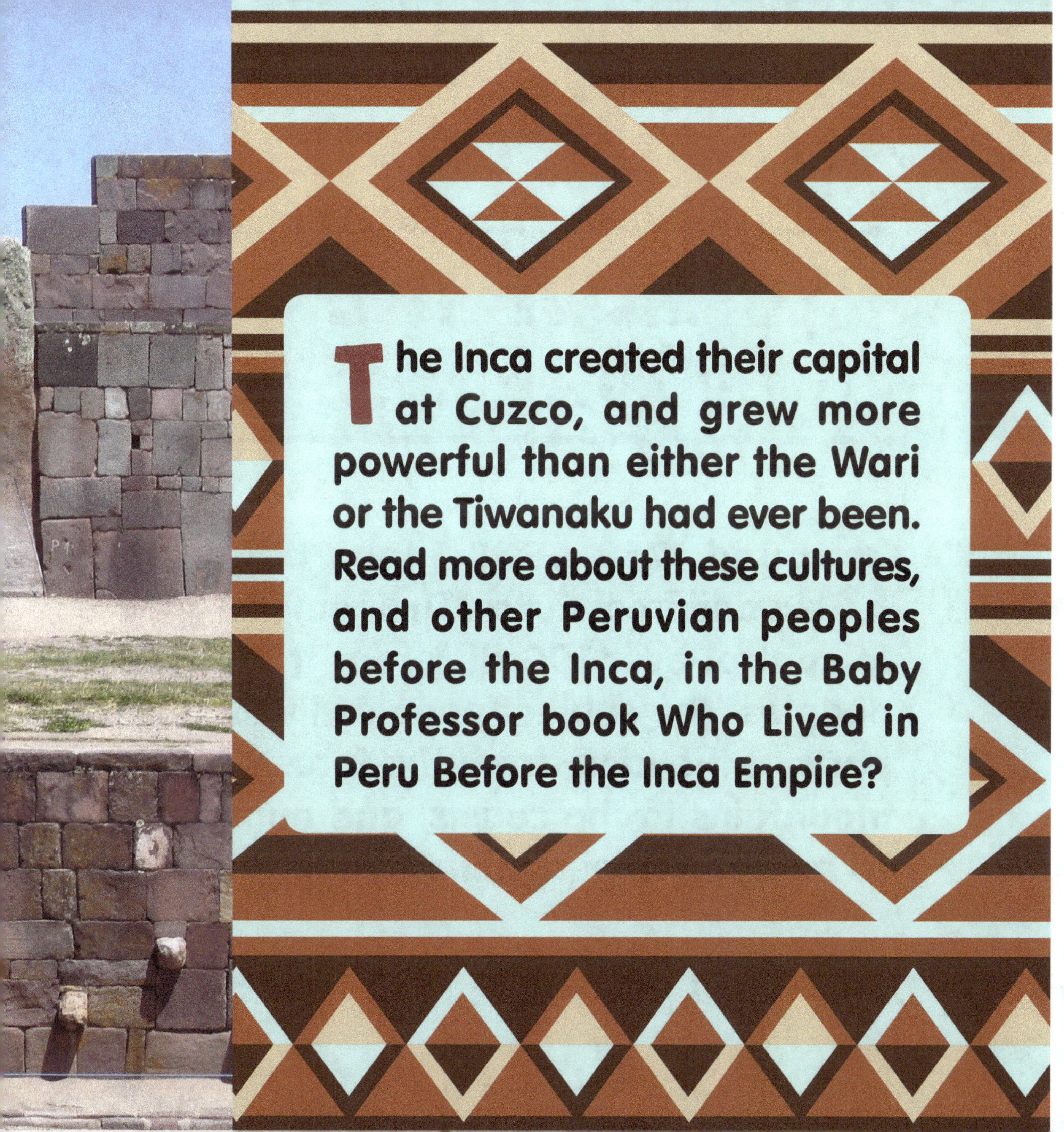

The Inca created their capital at Cuzco, and grew more powerful than either the Wari or the Tiwanaku had ever been. Read more about these cultures, and other Peruvian peoples before the Inca, in the Baby Professor book *Who Lived in Peru Before the Inca Empire?*

HOW THE EMPIRE GREW

Around 1250 CE the Inca began to expand from Cuzco. Their empire grew to control over 100 different tribes and peoples. The subject peoples lived in all parts of the land, from the forests to the mountains to the coasts, and numbered as many as fifteen million people.

PERUVIAN WITH TRADITIONAL CLOTHING

VIEW OF MACHU PICCHU INCA CITY AND SERPENTINE ROAD

As the empire grew, the Inca developed systems to control their many subjects. They built road networks to all the major centers of the empire. The roads let messengers carry information quickly, helped merchants move their goods, and let armies go to where they were needed. Some fragments of the road system are still in use. In all, there were more than six thousand miles of main roads, and over twenty thousand miles of trails and paths that led off from the main roads to villages, mines, and farming areas.

The conquered peoples provided the Inca with food like potatoes and corn; cotton; animals like alpaca and llamas; and goods as varied as pottery, tapestries, and objects made from silver and gold.

ALPACAS IN FIELD WALKING

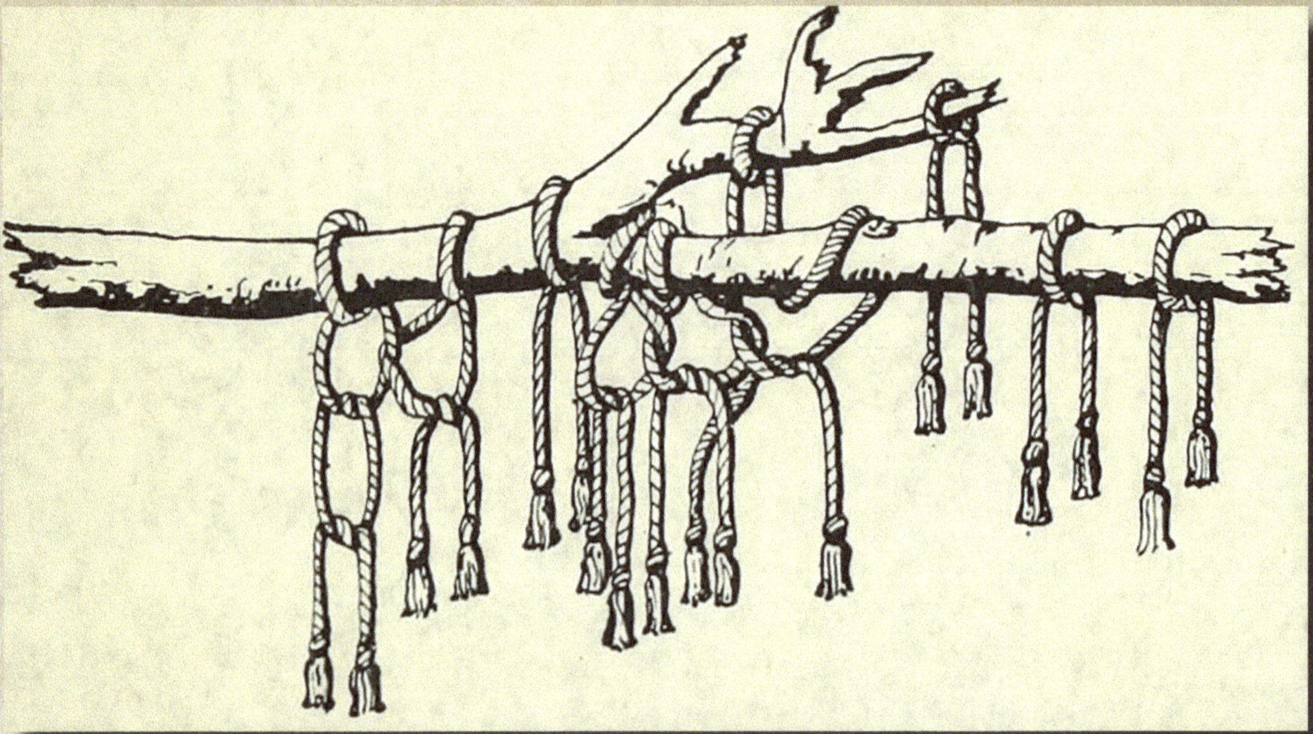

QUIPO

The Inca did not have a complex written language, but they had an accurate way of sending information. They tied patterns of knots in bundles of strings, known as "quipo", which messengers could carry to where the information needed to go. The people receiving the quipo knew how to read the pattern and could then act on the message that had been sent to them.

The Inca passed on other information, like the great deeds of their past kings or the legends of their people, in songs and in paintings.

DETAIL OF ANCIENT WALL AT HUACA DE LA LUNA IN TRUJILLO, PERU

Atarmango Capac Primer Rey Del Cuzco:

THE INCA RULERS

The rulers of the empire were part of a complicated extended set of family relationships called the ayllu system. An ayllu could include thousands of people. Where you fit in your ayllu controlled your access to land, whom you could marry, what powers you would have, and what role you would play in important religious ceremonies.

The supreme ruler of the Inca had the title "capac". All the capacs, by tradition, came from the same extended family. In Inca legend, the first rulers were four brothers and four sisters who came out of a cave at Pacaritambo.

MANCO CAPAC WATER FOUNTAIN GOLDEN STATUE

UNIQUE ANCIENT INCA CIRCULAR TERRACES

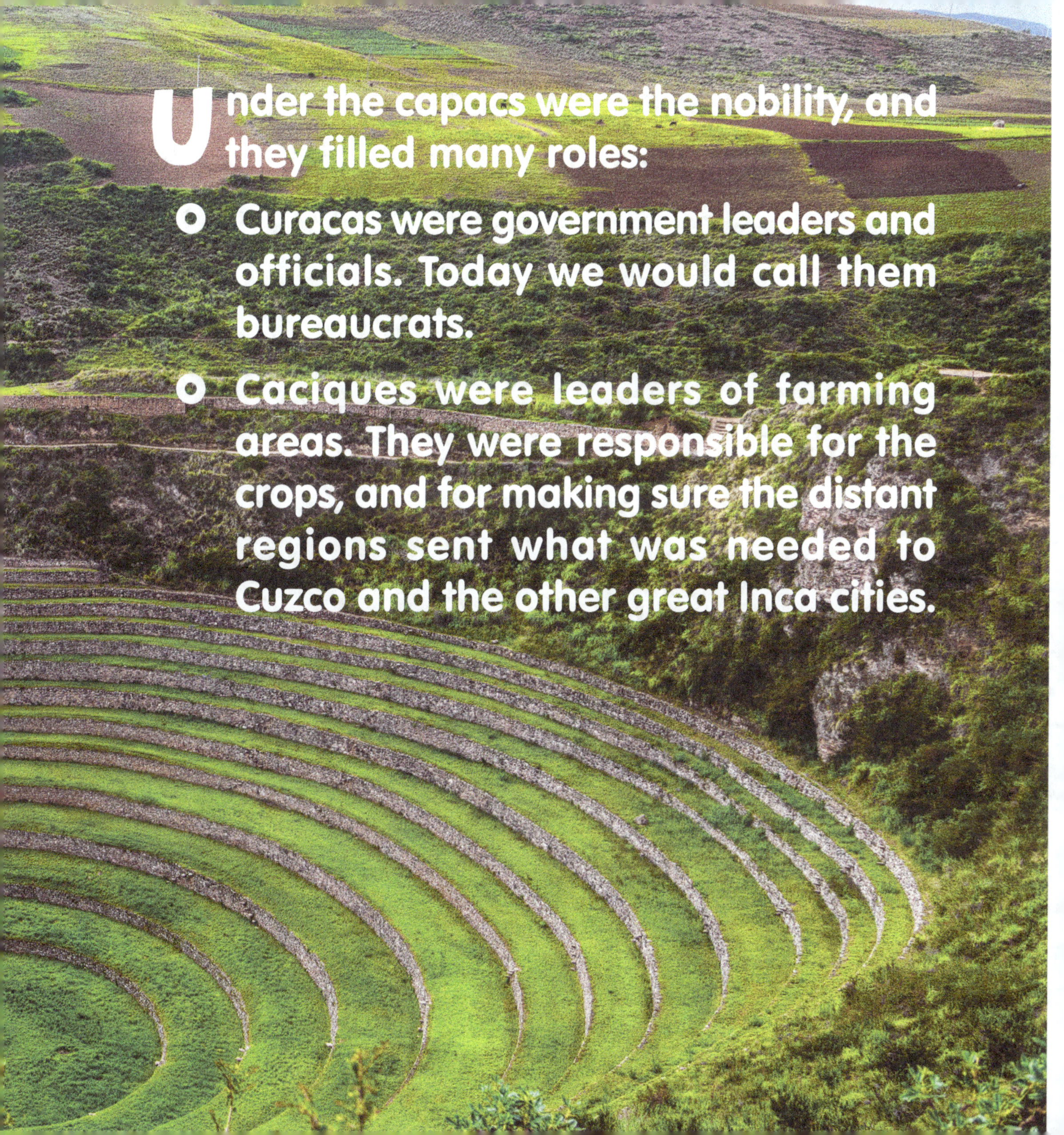

Under the capacs were the nobility, and they filled many roles:

- Curacas were government leaders and officials. Today we would call them bureaucrats.

- Caciques were leaders of farming areas. They were responsible for the crops, and for making sure the distant regions sent what was needed to Cuzco and the other great Inca cities.

- **Chasqui were-highly trained messengers. They could run great distances to carry information across the empire, making use of the road system and of a series of outposts or rest stations. Travelling on foot, without carts or horses to help them, a series of chasqui could send a message almost two hundred miles in a day.**

CHASQUI

QUECHUA LADIES AND A YOUNG BOY CHATTING ON AN ANCIENT INCA WALL, PERU.

Here are some great things to know about the Inca Empire:

- Another name for the Inca Empire is "Tawantinsuyu", which means "all four parts together".

- The official language of the empire was Quecha, which the Inca called "people speech", or "runasimi".

- **The Inca were the first people to grow many plants we now eat all around the world, like the potato. They were thoughtful farmers, building canals to bring water to the fields and using natural fertilizers like manure to make the soil richer.**

THE MARKET AT PISAC, IN THE URUBAMBA VALLEY NEAR CUSCO,
FEATURES A WIDE VARIETY OF FRUITS AND VEGETABLES.

MACHU PICCHU, WONDER OF THE WORLD, TEMPLE OF THE SUN

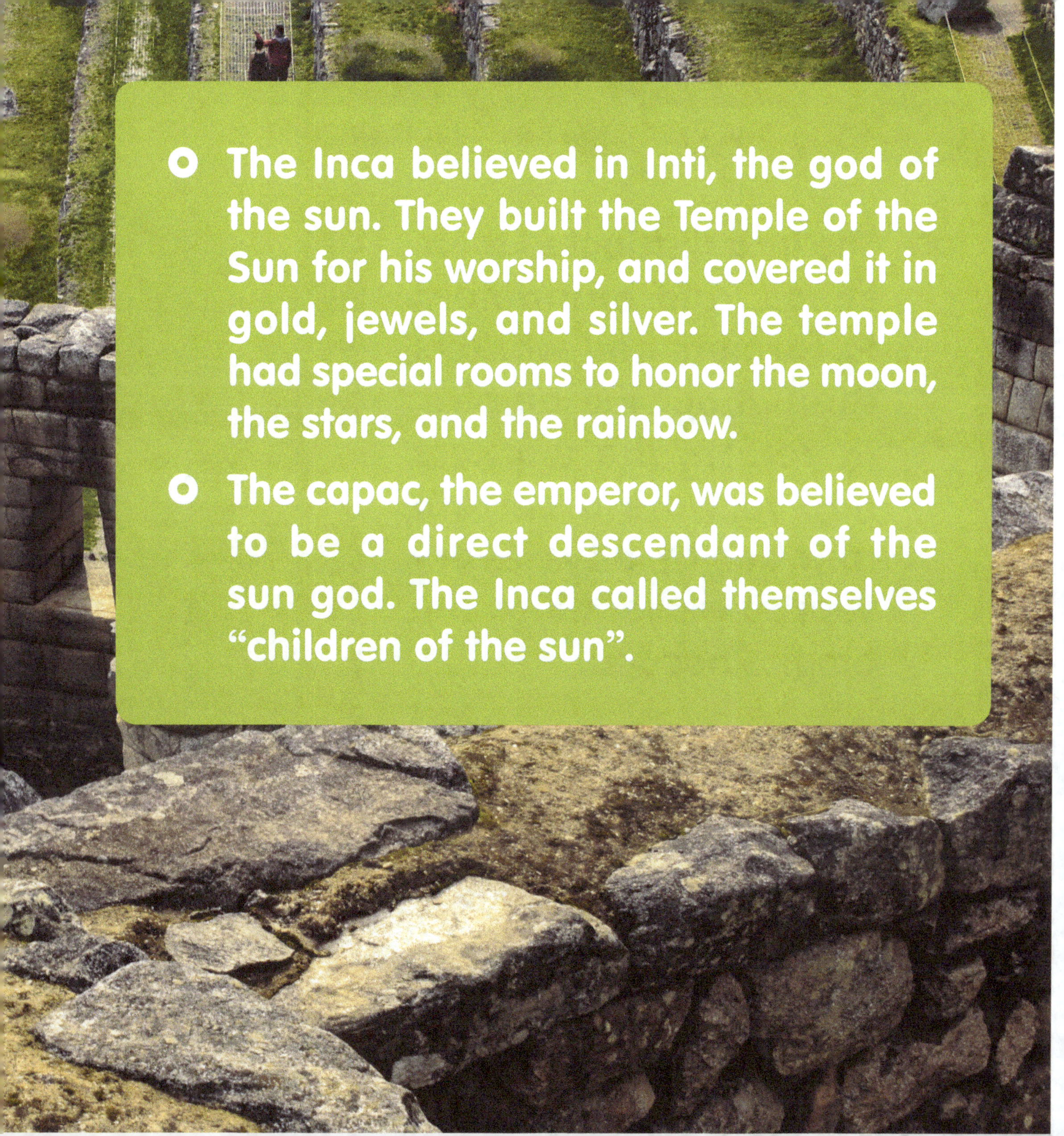

The Inca believed in Inti, the god of the sun. They built the Temple of the Sun for his worship, and covered it in gold, jewels, and silver. The temple had special rooms to honor the moon, the stars, and the rainbow.

The capac, the emperor, was believed to be a direct descendant of the sun god. The Inca called themselves "children of the sun".

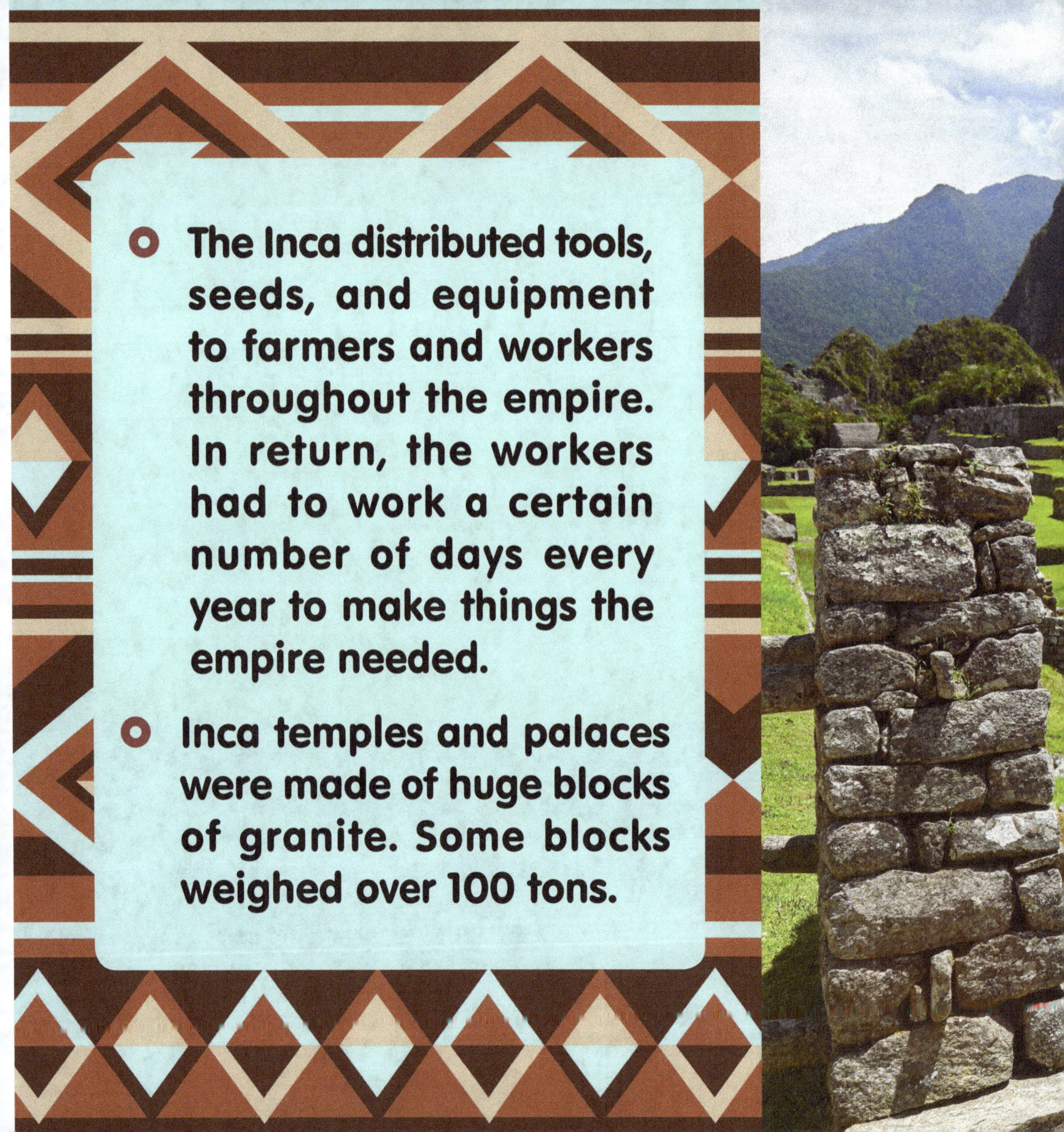

- **The Inca distributed tools, seeds, and equipment to farmers and workers throughout the empire. In return, the workers had to work a certain number of days every year to make things the empire needed.**

- **Inca temples and palaces were made of huge blocks of granite. Some blocks weighed over 100 tons.**

MACHU PICCHU ANCIENT TEMPLE INCA IN PERU.

SCULPTURE OF THE SUN GOD

- The Inca religion taught that people could be reborn after dying. If a person followed the code of the Inca—to tell the truth, not steal, and work hard—the sun god would reward him with a new life. Those who did not follow the code would lie forever in the cold ground.

- The babies of the nobility had their heads wrapped tightly with cloth while they were small. The bones of the skull then developed into a cone shape, rather than a round skull. If you had a cone-shaped head it showed everyone you were part of the ruling class.

THE END OF THE EMPIRE

The Inca built their empire by conquest, defeating many other peoples and nations. Many of those people were unhappy to be part of the empire, so there were many rebellions. The army was often busy, moving along the road system to enforce the will of the empire on its different tribes. On top of that, there was a split in the nobility, with open war to see who would be the capac.

INCA ARMY

SICK KID WITH MEASLES

Another factor was disease. The Europeans brought smallpox, measles, and other diseases to the new world, and the Native Americans had little resistance against them. Devastating epidemics killed up to half the population in some areas and disrupted the economy and society.

When Francisco Pizarro led 160 Spanish fighters into the Inca Empire in 1532, the capac, Atahualpa, had an army of tens of thousands of fighters at his command. But the Spaniards had armor, guns, cannons, and horses, none of which the Inca had seen before. The Spaniards also sprung a trap, killing thousands of Inca fighters in one battle and capturing, and later killing, Atahualpa.

EXECUTION OF THE LAST INCAN EMPEROR, ATAHUALLPA
BY SPANISH CONQUISTADOR, FRANCISCO PIZZARO

PIZARRO'S TROOPS

Once further troops arrived, Pizarro marched on the capital, Cuzco, and captured it without a fight in 1533. Pizarro declared himself the governor of what had been Inca territory. In 1536 there was a final Inca uprising, which did not succeed. That marked the end of the Inca Empire.

Learn More About the Inca Empire

There is much more to learn about the Inca Empire and the region. Try Baby Professor books like Inca Government and Society and The Two Major Cities of the Inca Empire: Cuzco and Machu Picchu.

INCA ECONOMICS

INTOXICANTS: Coca, chicha (maize beer)

MARKETS: A widespread trade network facilitated by open markets

CULTIVATED CROPS: Cotton, potatoes, maize, quinoa

RED QUINOA SEEDS IN WOODEN BOWL.

GUINEA PIG EATING BASIL

DOMESTICATED ANIMALS: Alpaca, llama, guinea pig

Tribute was paid to Cusco in goods and services; tribute tallies were kept on quipu and an annual census was kept including the number of deaths and births

LAPIDARY ARTS: Shell

METALLURGY: Silver, copper, tin and to a lesser extent gold were cold-hammered, forged, and air-annealed

METALLURGY PRODUCT

TEXTILES: Wool (alpaca and llama) and cotton

AGRICULTURE: When necessary in the steep Andean terrain, the Inca built terraces with a gravel base and stepped retaining walls, to drain excess water and allow water flow from the terrace tread to the next terrace downslope.

TRADITIONAL QUECHUAN ALPACA WEAVING TOOLS AND BALLS OF ALPACA YARN

TEXTURE OF MUD BRICK WALL

INCA ARCHITECTURE

Construction techniques used by the Inca included fired adobe mud bricks, roughly shaped stones interspersed with mud mortar, and large, finely shaped stones coated with mud and clay finishing. The shaped stone architecture (sometimes called 'pillow-faced') is among the finest in the world, with large stones sanded into tight jigsaw like patterns.

Pillow-faced architecture was reserved for temples, administrative structures and royal residences like Machu Picchu.

Many Inca military installations and other public architecture were constructed throughout the empire, at sites such as Farfán (Peru), Qara Qara and Yampara (Bolivia), and Catarpe and Turi (Chile).

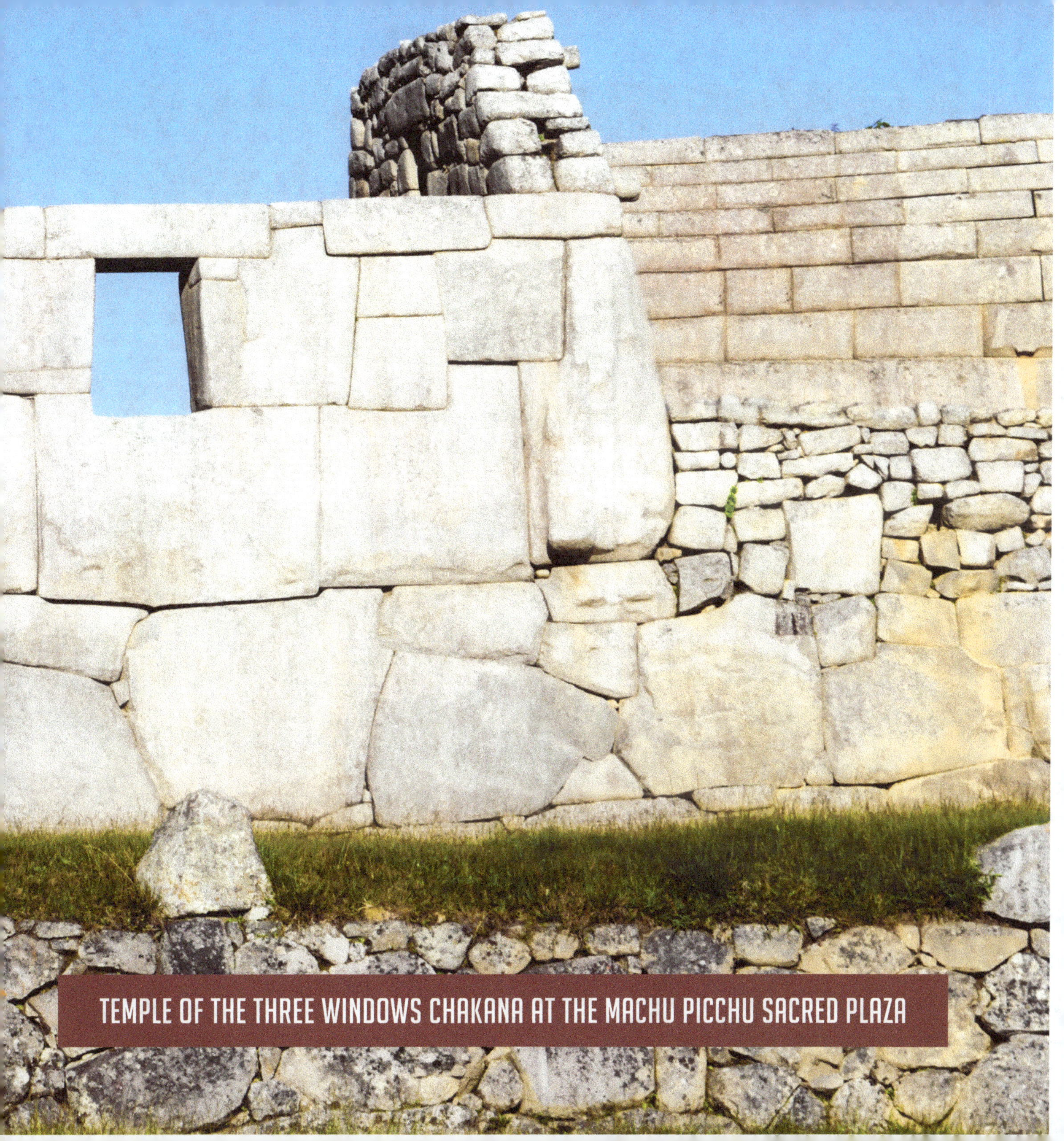

TEMPLE OF THE THREE WINDOWS CHAKANA AT THE MACHU PICCHU SACRED PLAZA

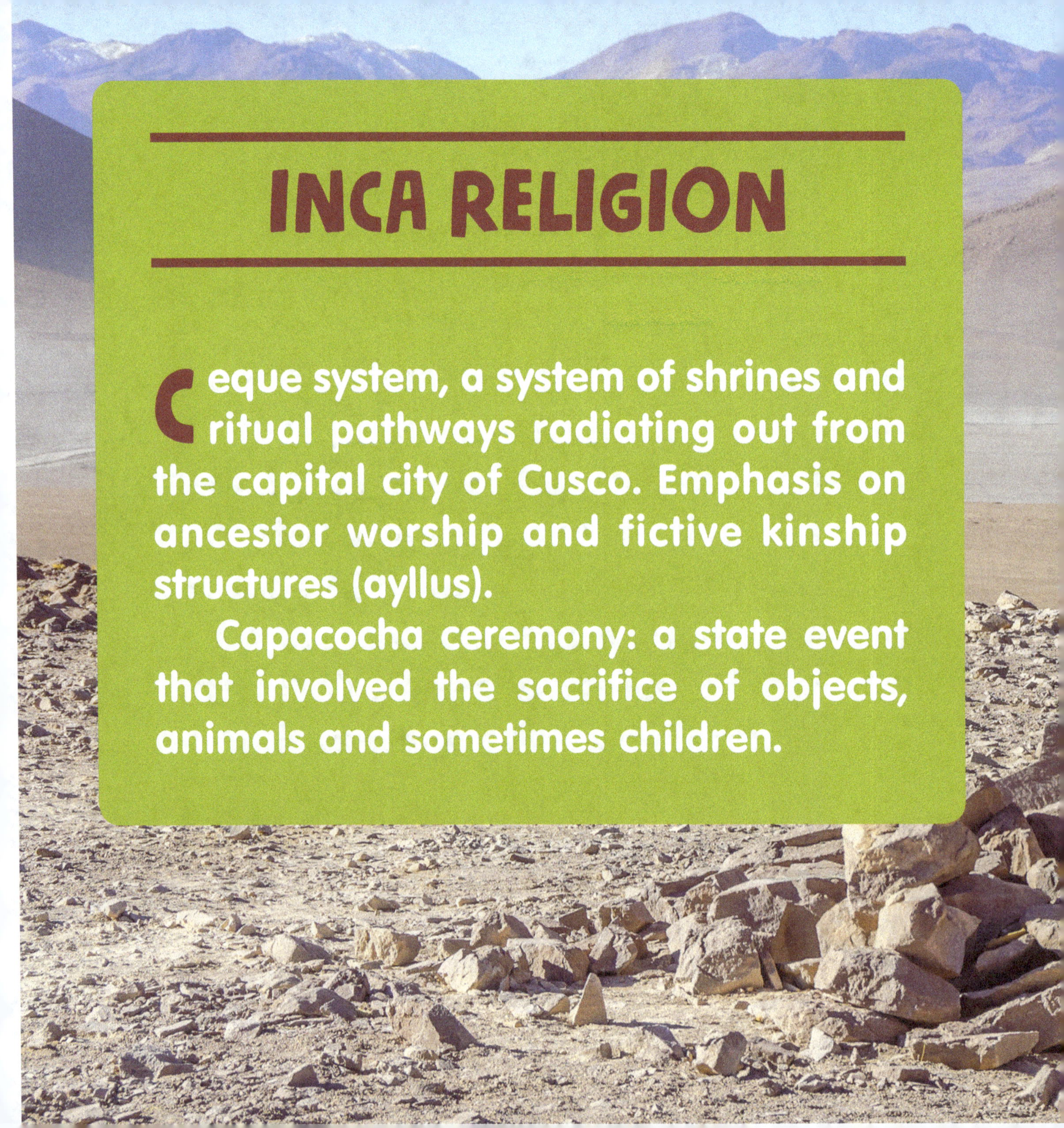

INCA RELIGION

Ceque system, a system of shrines and ritual pathways radiating out from the capital city of Cusco. Emphasis on ancestor worship and fictive kinship structures (ayllus).

Capacocha ceremony: a state event that involved the sacrifice of objects, animals and sometimes children.

CAIRN, QUECHUAN SHRINE TO THE INDIGENOUS INCA GODDESS PACHAMAMA

CHAUCHILLA ANCIENT CEMETERY IN THE DESERT OF NAZCA, PERU

Burials: The Inca dead were mummified and placed in open sepulchers so that they could be disinterred for important annual ceremonies and other rituals.

Temples/shrines known as 'huacas' included both built and natural structures

Visit
BABY PROFESSOR
EDUCATION KIDS
www.BabyProfessorBooks.com
to download Free Baby Professor eBooks
and view our catalog of new and exciting
Children's Books